I0003666

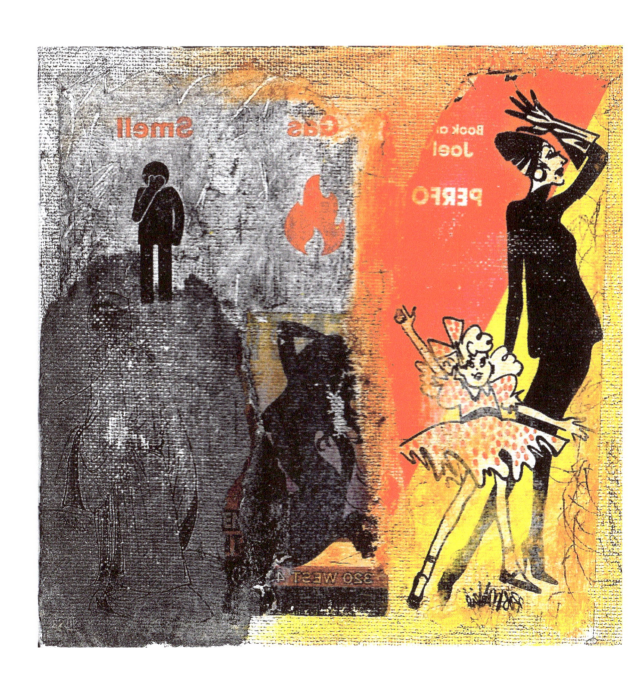

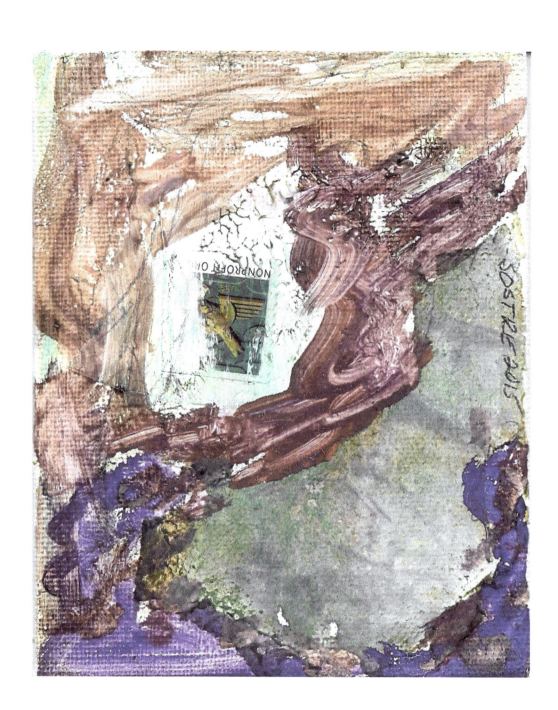

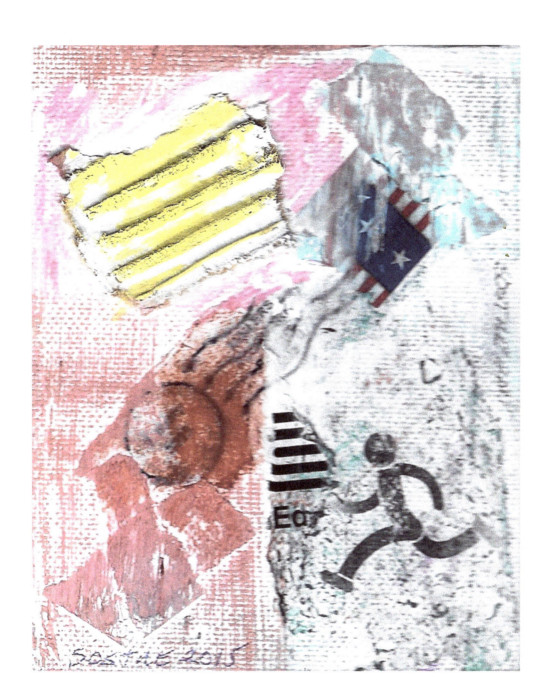

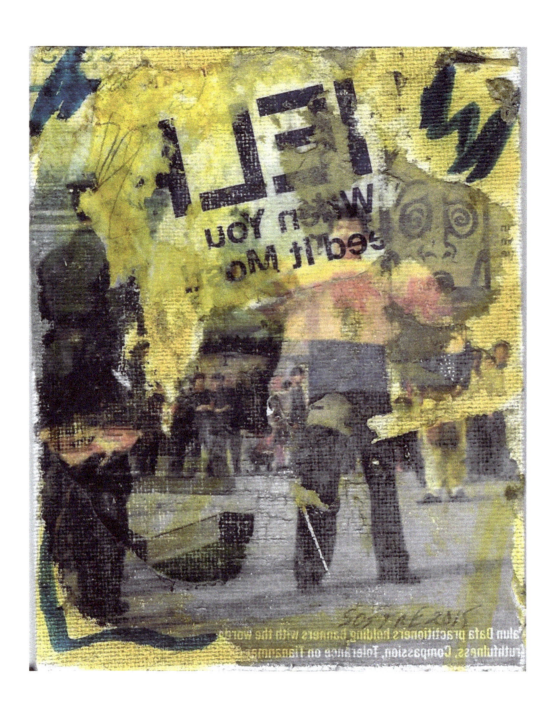

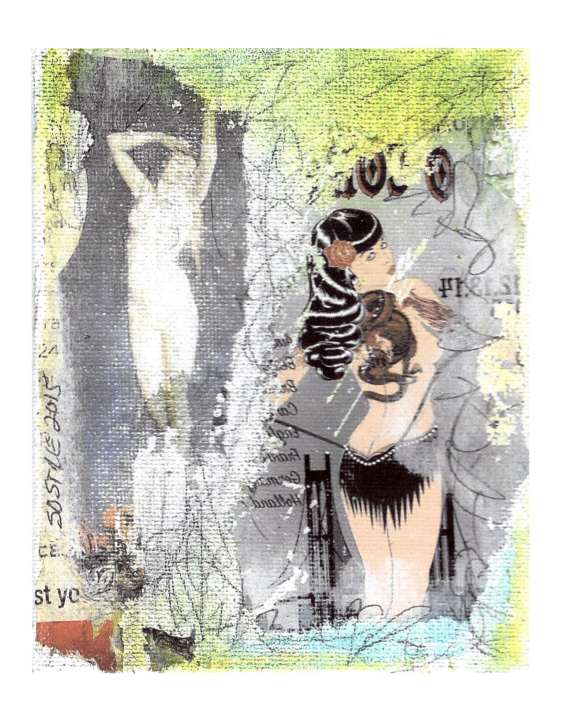

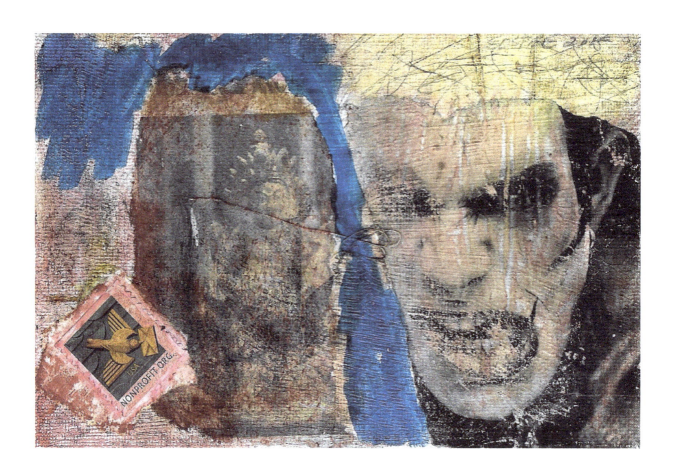

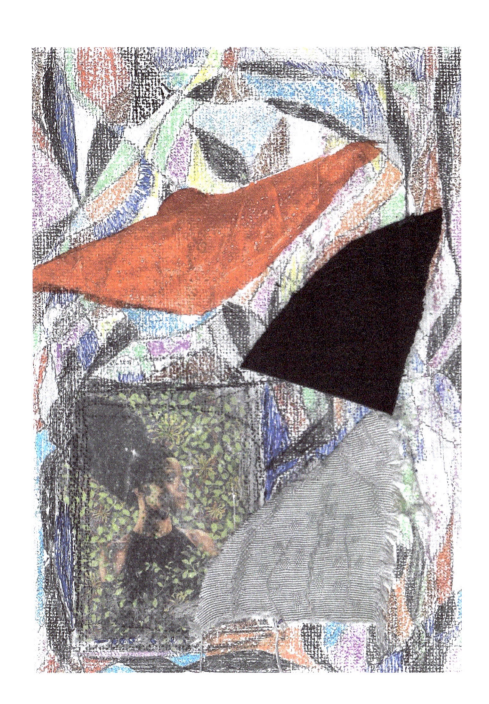

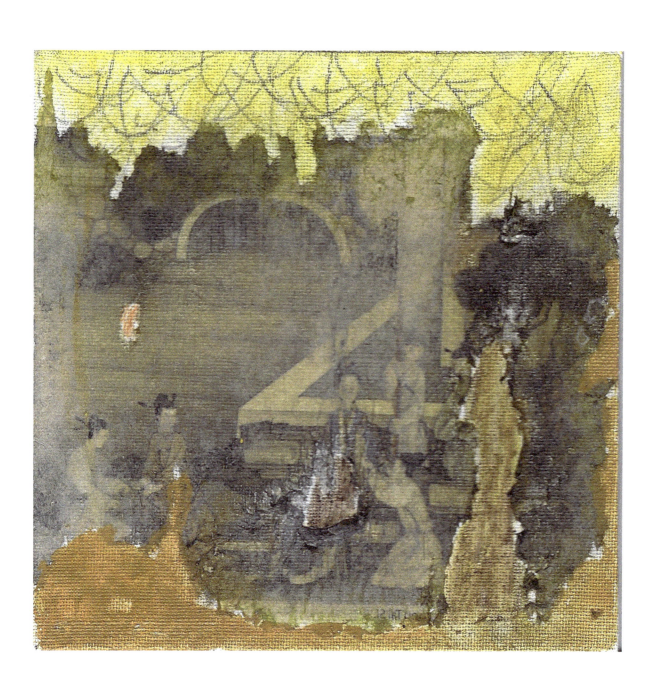

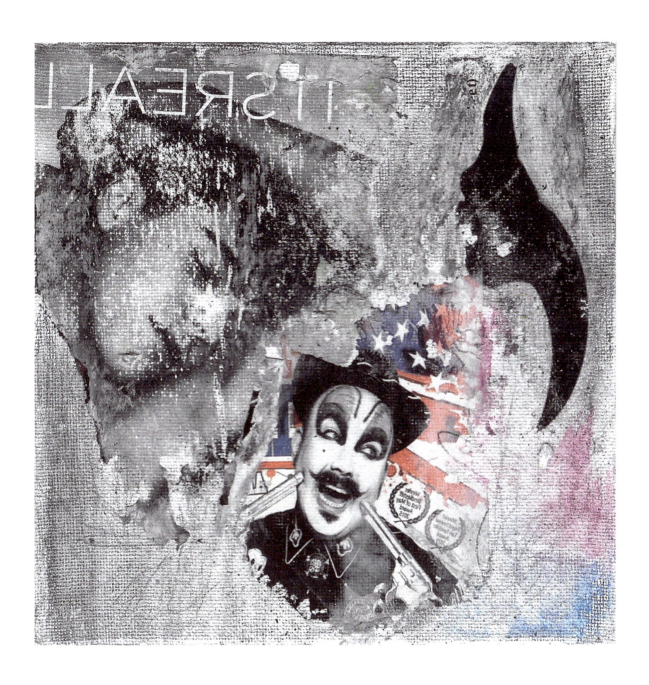

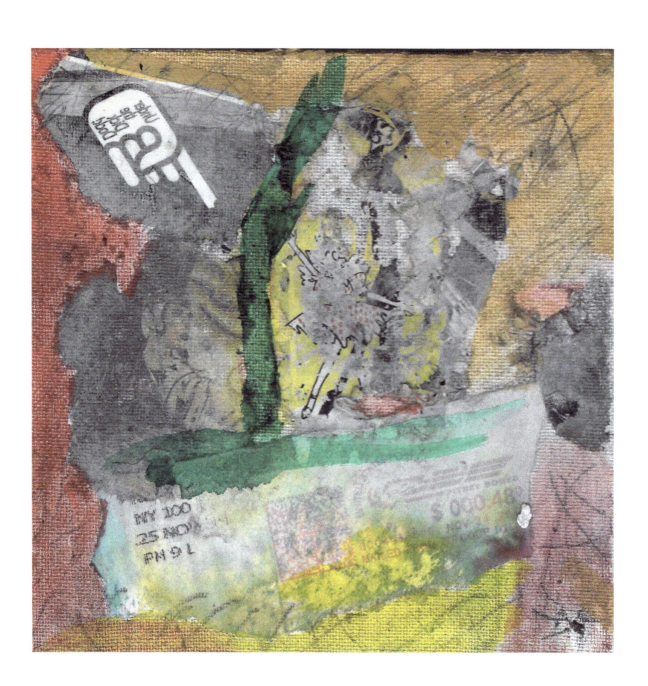

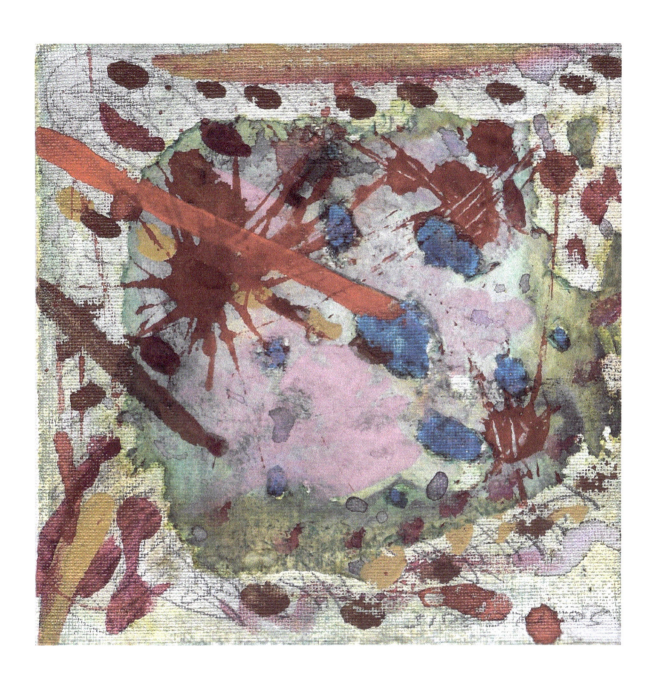

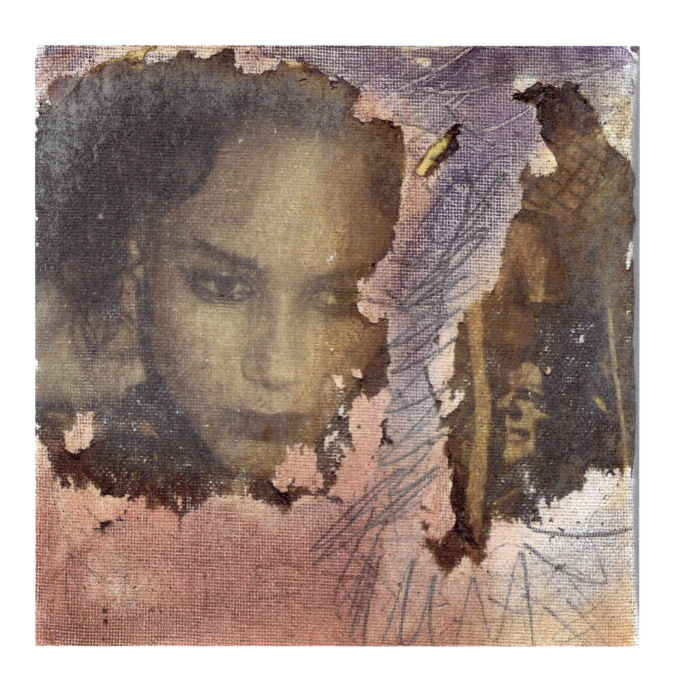

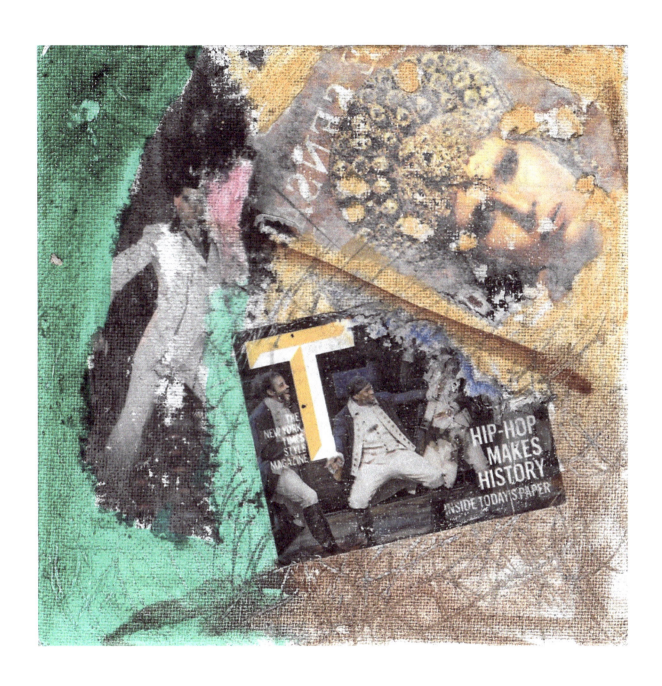

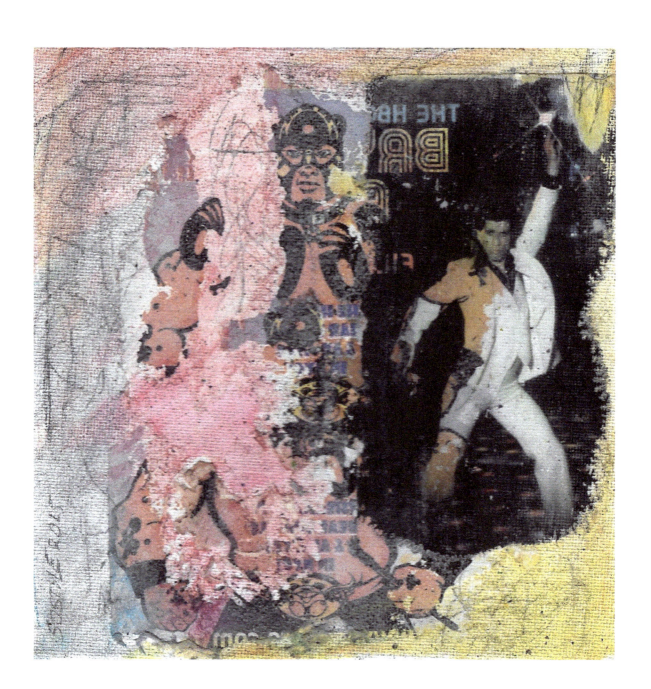

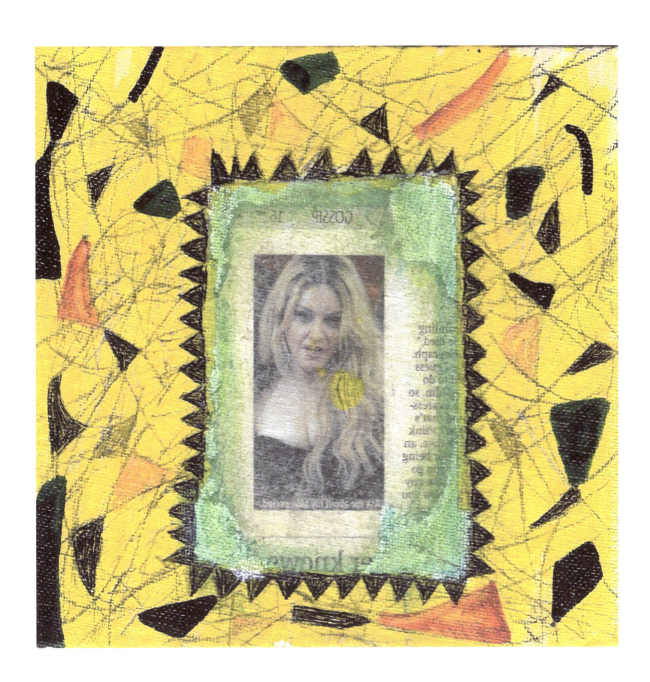

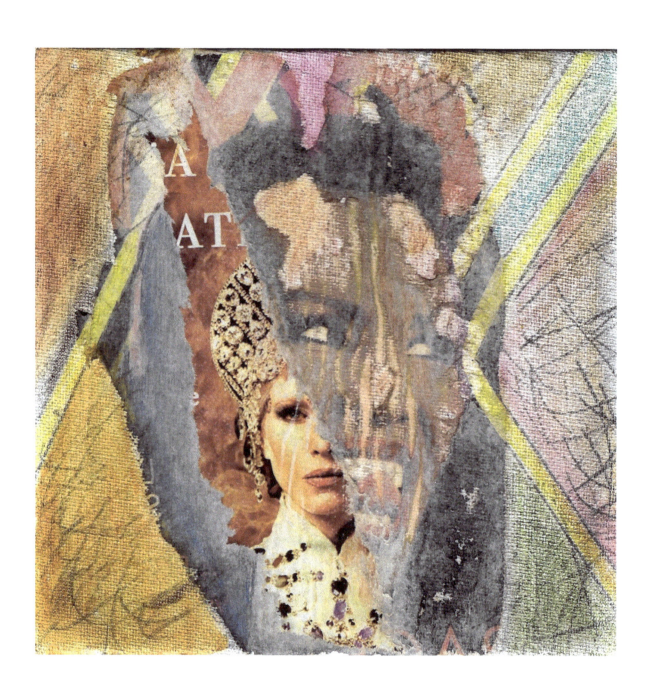

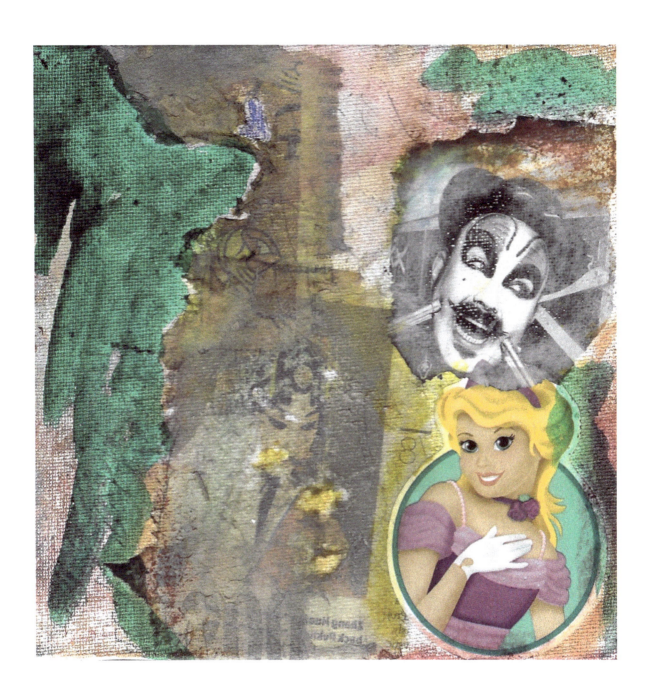

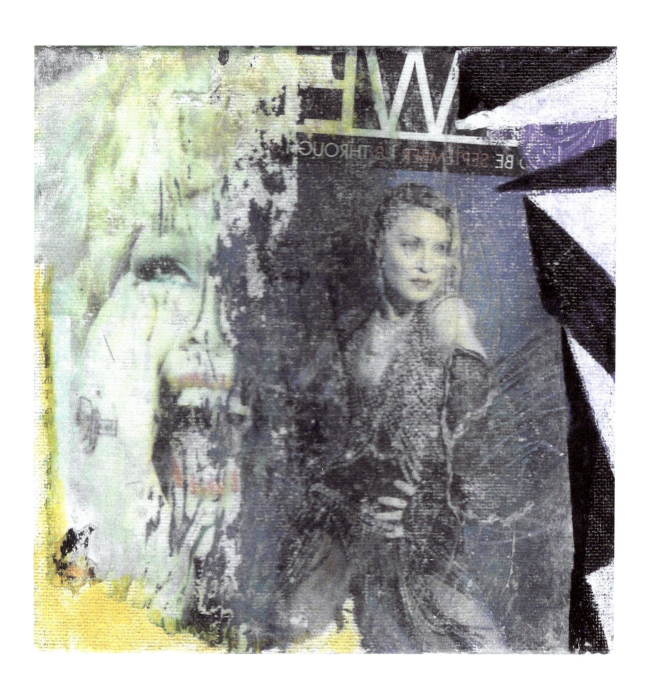

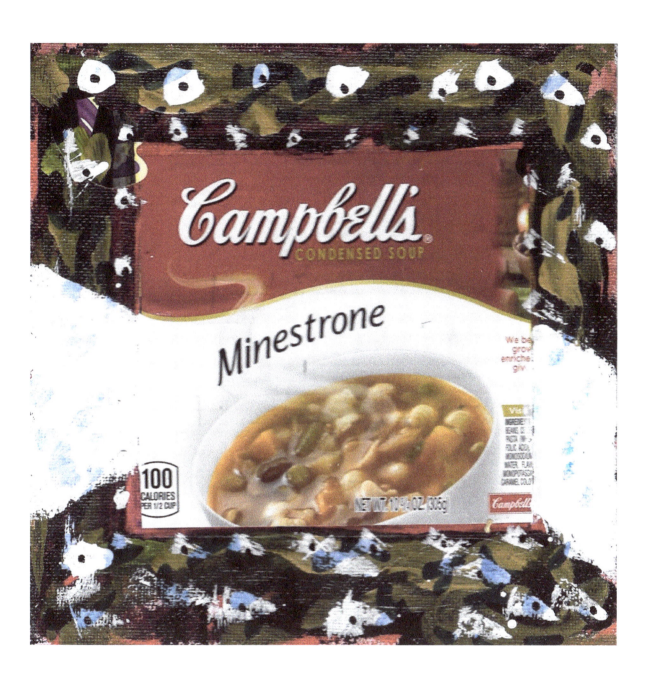

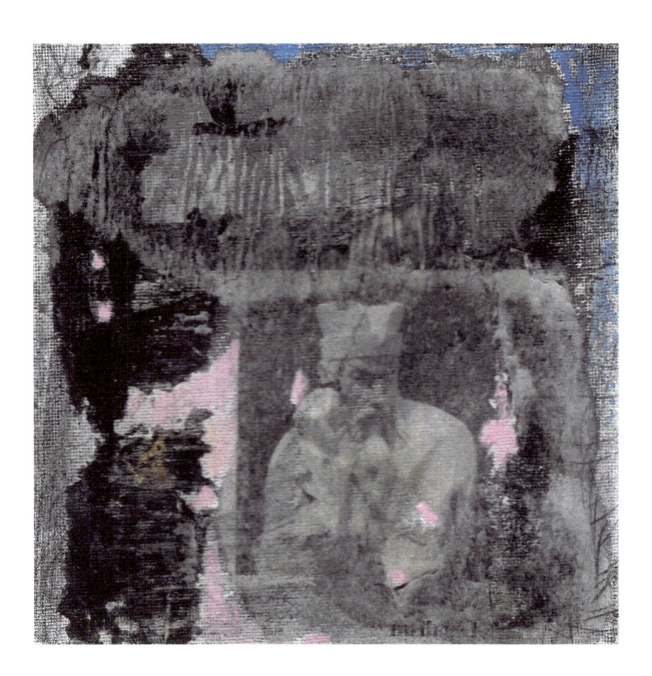

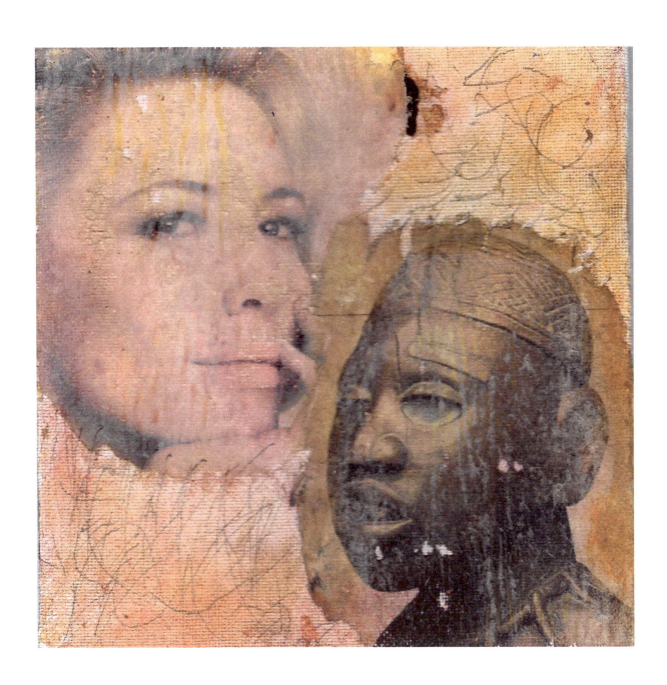

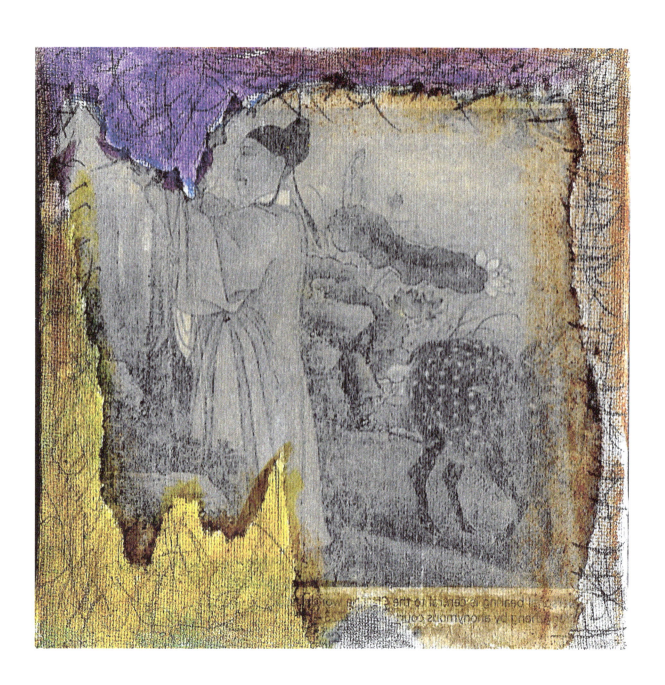

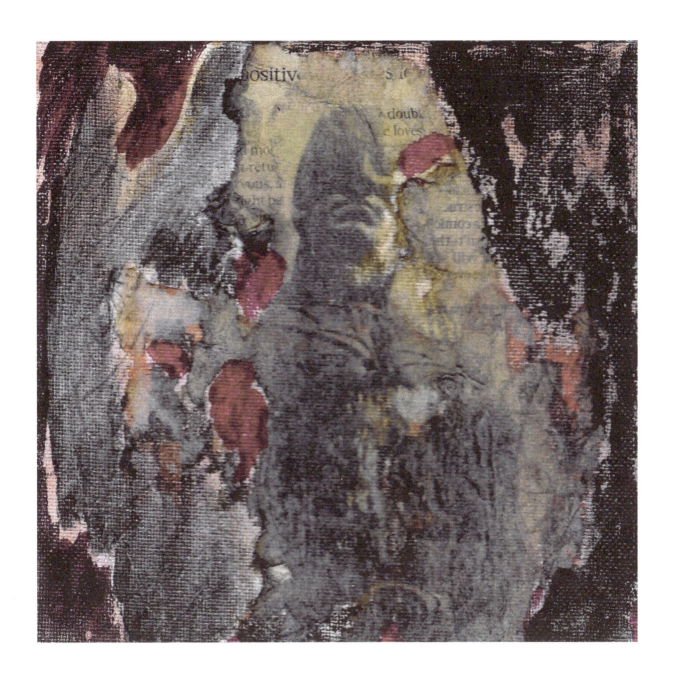

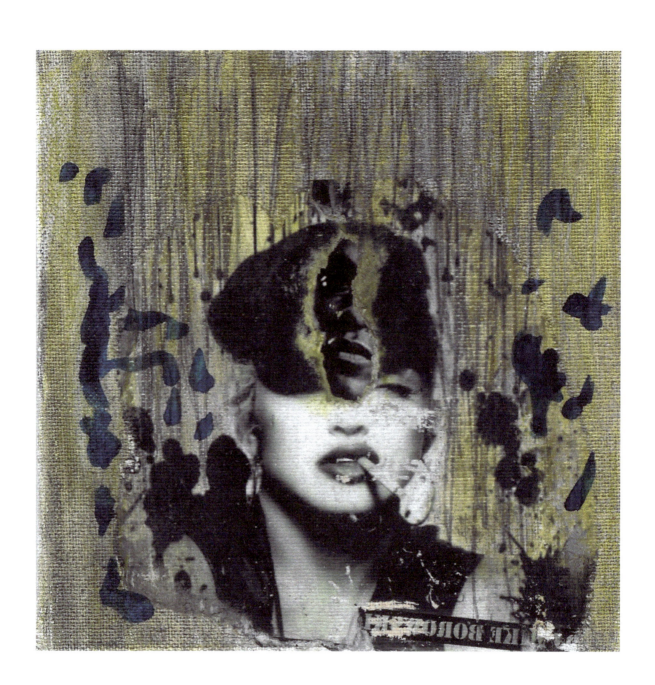

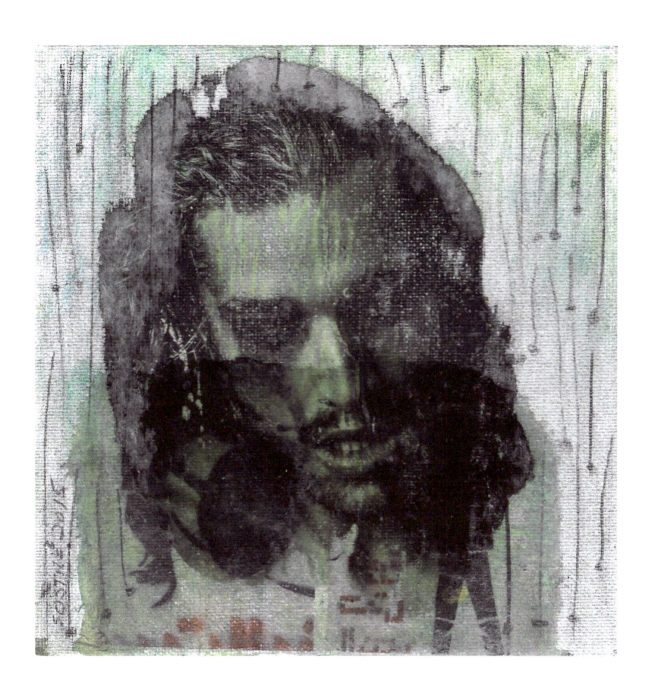

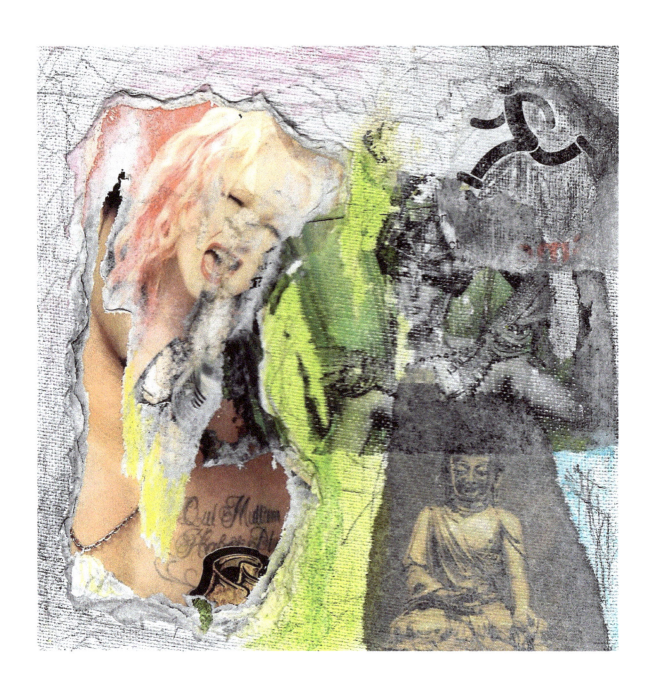

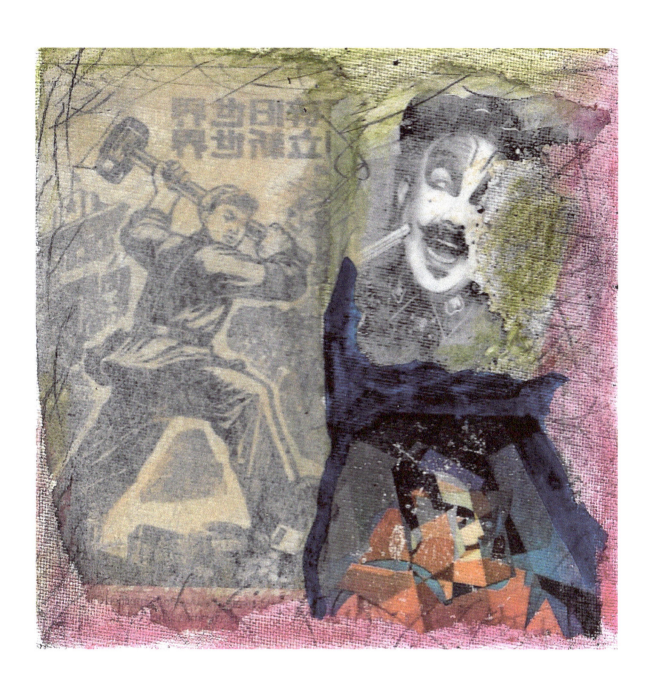

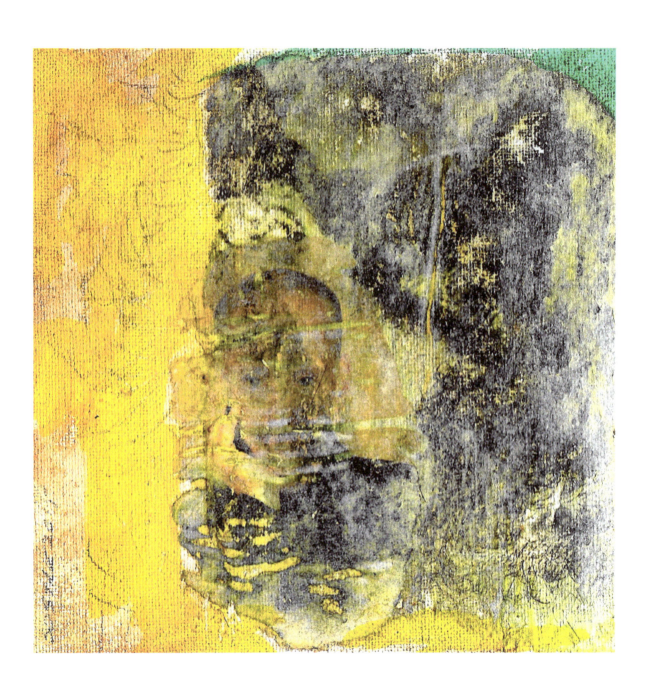

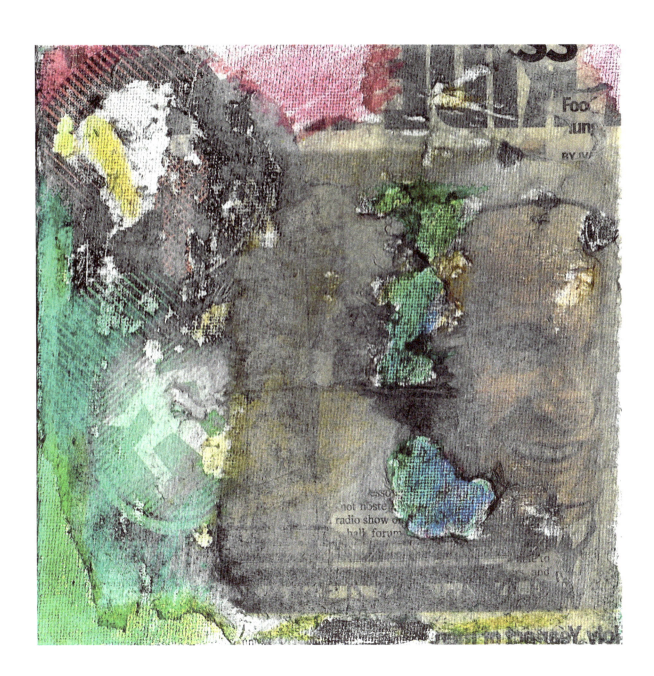

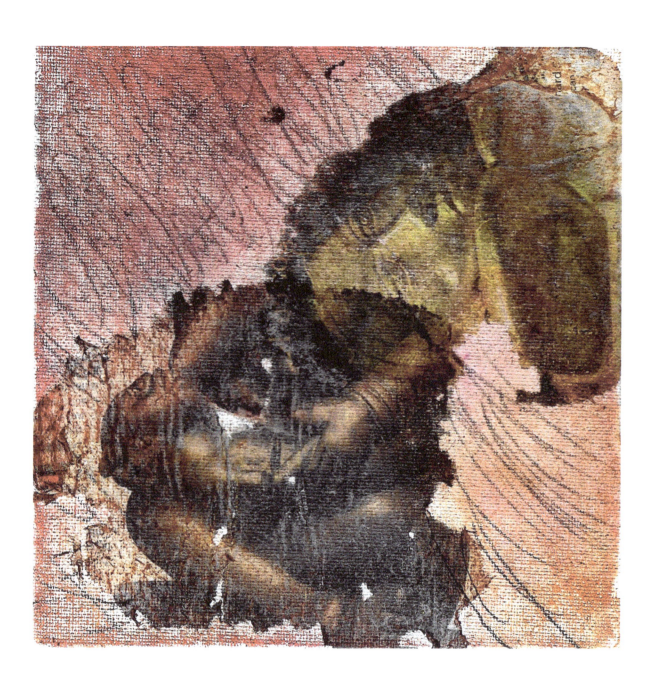

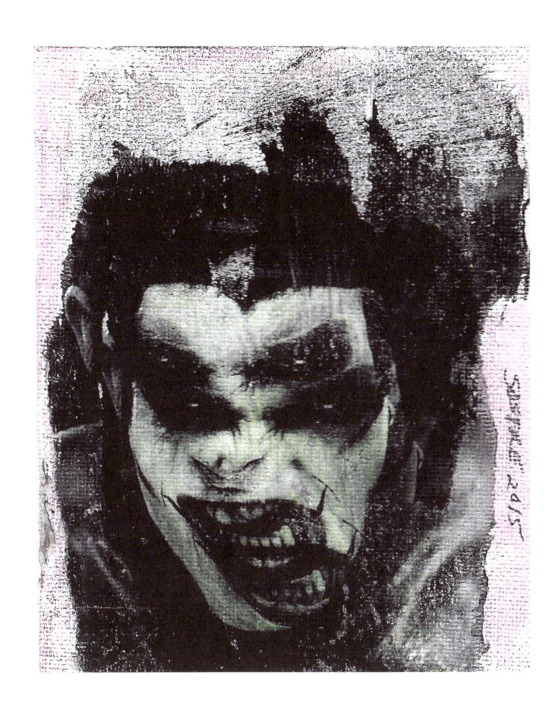

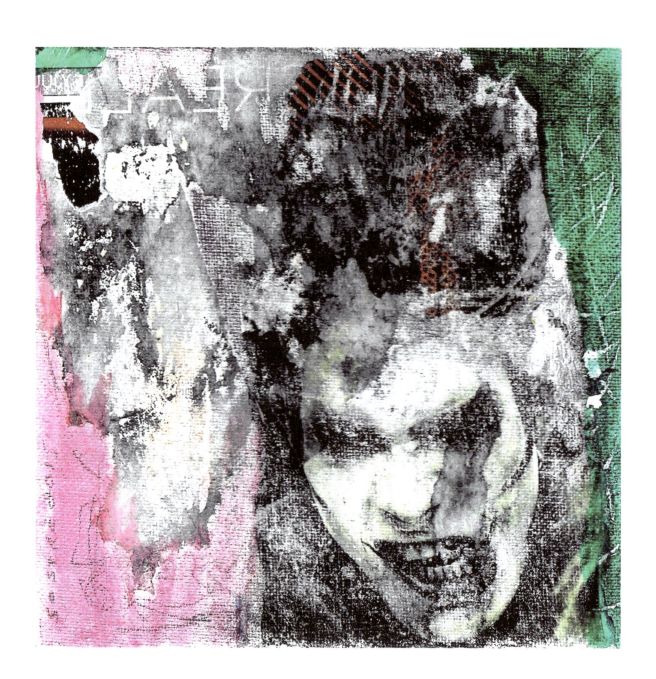

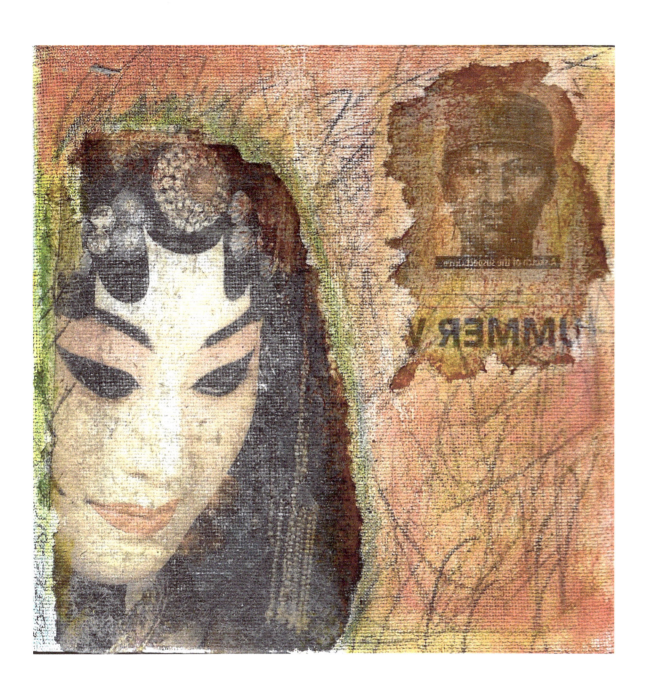

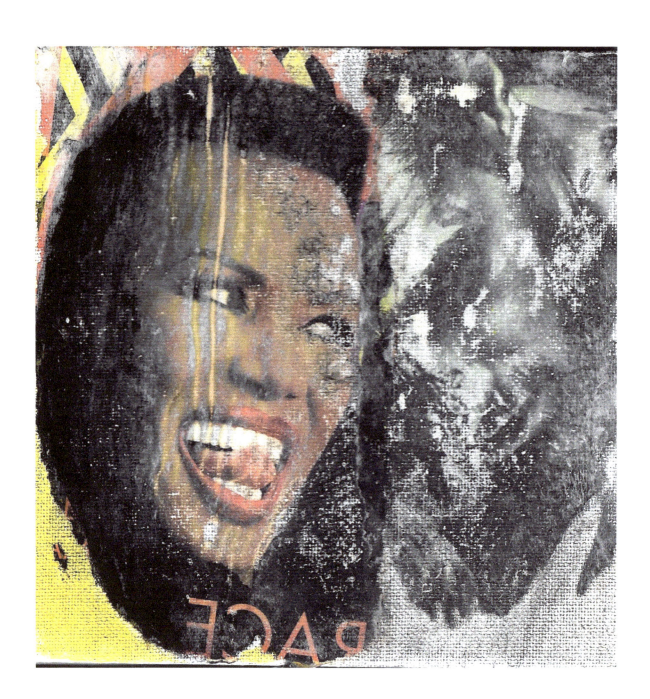

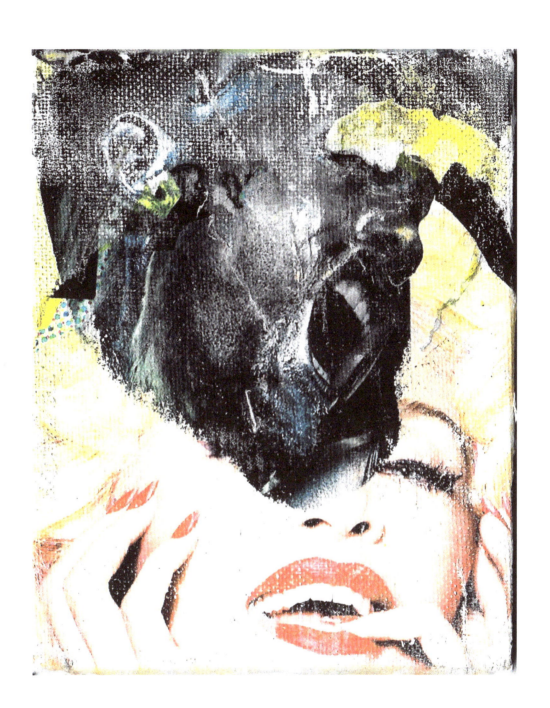

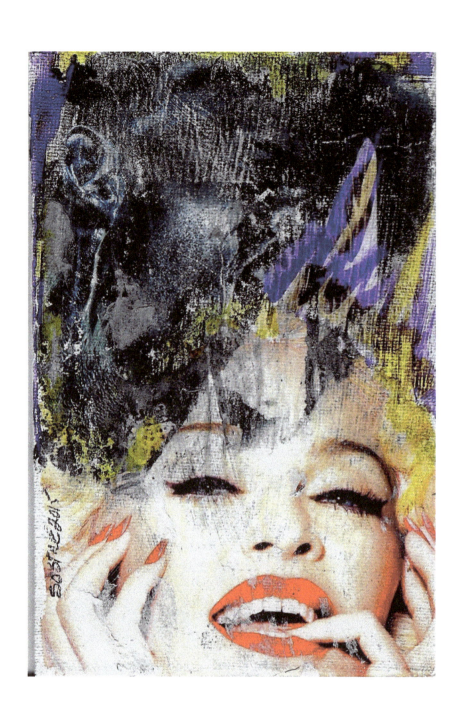

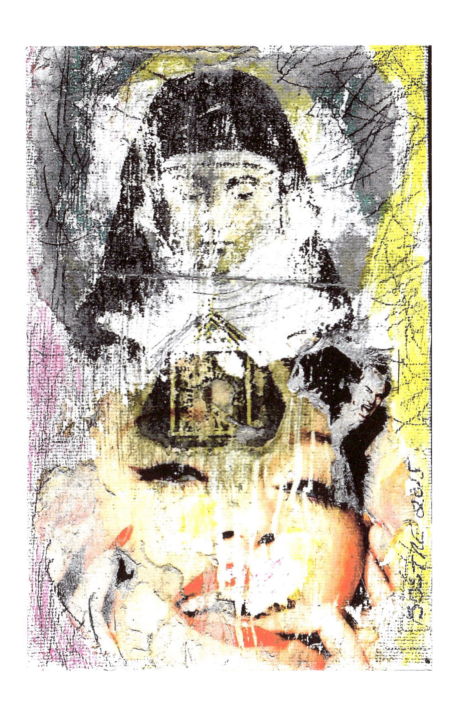

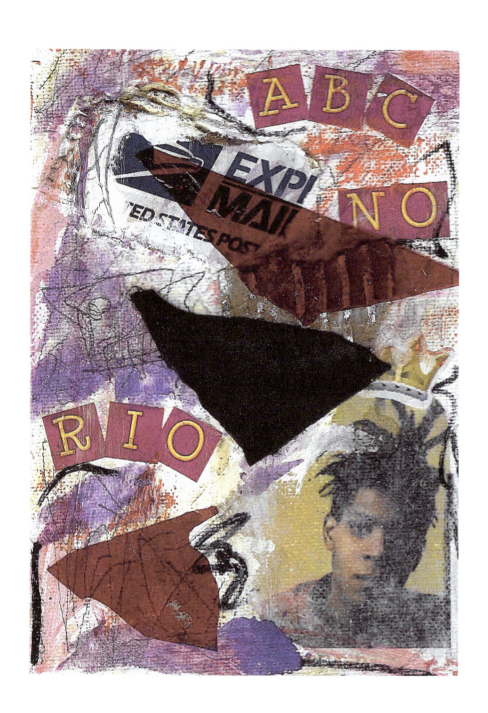

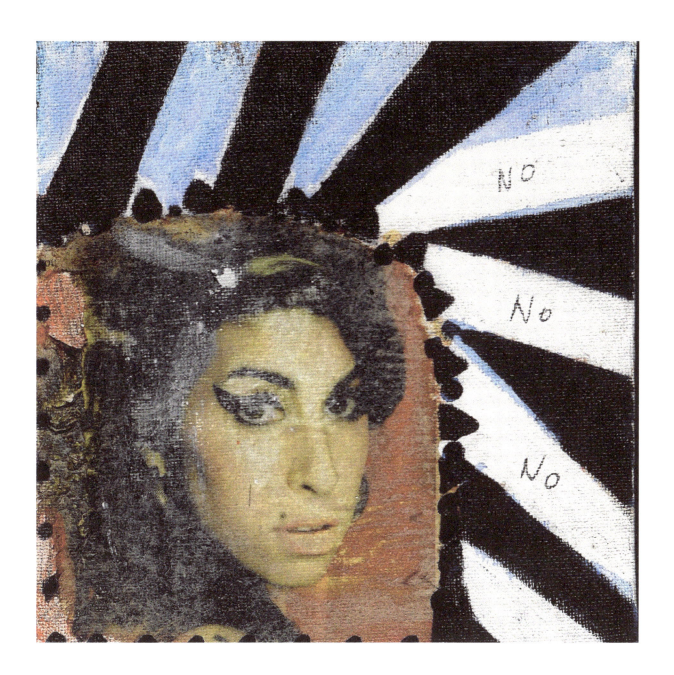

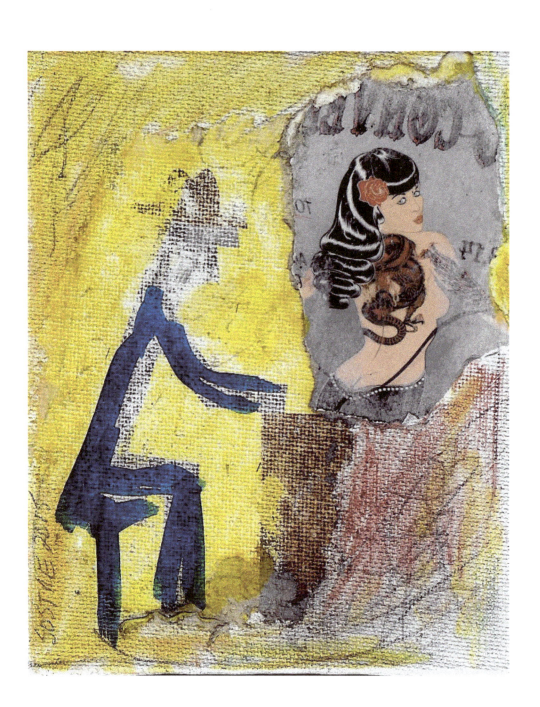

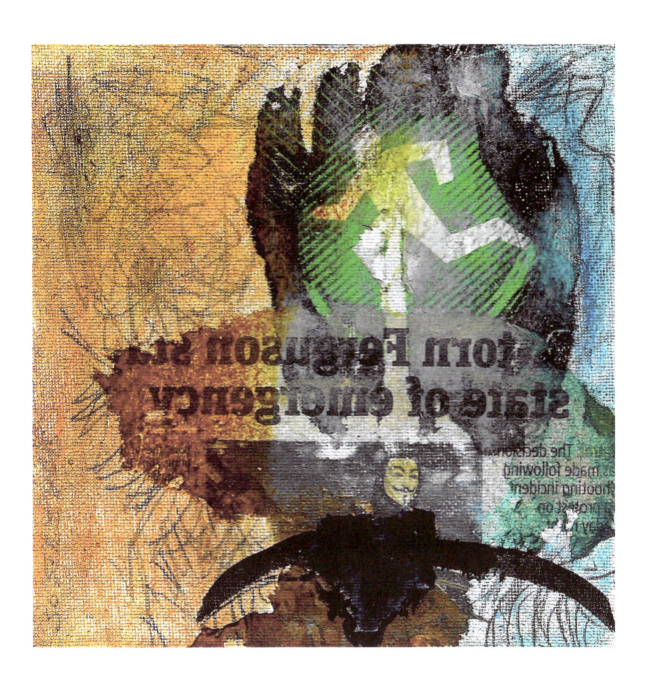

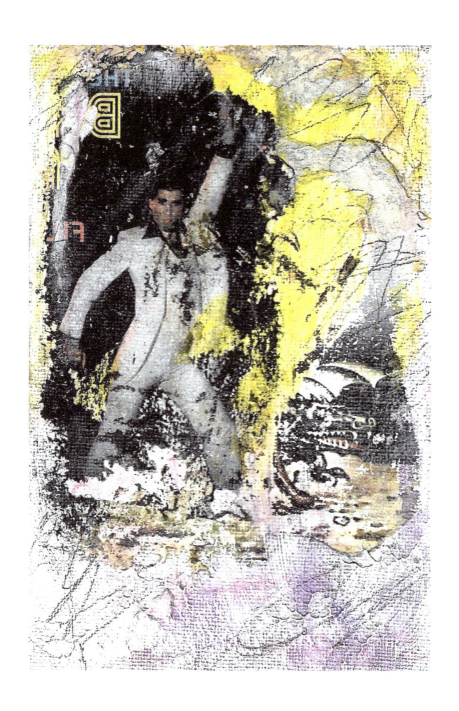

2015 all works are acrylic, craypas, pencil, gel
image transfer on 4x6 inch canvas board.

www.ingramcontent.com/pod-product-compliance
Lightning Source LLC
LaVergne TN
LVHW061953050326
832904LV00010B/302